Animal
Planet®

SNAKES!

Face-to-Face

Keep up with all the great adventures,
and don't miss a single experience!

SNAKES!
Face-to-Face

by Jane Hammerslough

Based on the Animal Planet program
The Jeff Corwin Experience

SCHOLASTIC INC.

New York   Toronto   London   Auckland   Sydney

Mexico City   New Delhi   Hong Kong   Buenos Aires

ISBN 0-439-43564-1

12 11 10 9 8 7 6 5 4 3   3 4 5 6 7 8/0

Printed in the U.S.A.
First printing, January 2003

Table of Contents

If you come across a word in the text that you don't understand, be sure to check out the Glossary on page 71 to see what it means.

If you're interested in snakes, you've come to the right place. Jeff Corwin and the *Experience* crew are about to embark on a journey to some incredible destinations all over the world. The goal? To experience some of the world's most amazing serpents!

Some can slither in sand, while others can swim through the ocean. Some can rattle, while others can hiss as loud as a dog can growl. Some are smaller than a pencil, while others grow to be longer than 30 feet. And while some are harmless, others can kill an elephant with a single bite!

From enormous anacondas in the South American country of Ecuador to the deadly, swift, African black mamba, from dangerous rattlesnakes to graceful vine snakes, the variety of serpents is extraordinary. Throughout the world, there are more than 2,700 types of snakes!

And thanks to *The Jeff Corwin Experience*, you can get up close and personal with these fascinating reptiles. Meeting them in ways you never have before is as easy as reading this book. From Southeast Asian jungles to Southwest American deserts, from African plains to South American rain forests, he's searching out serpents . . . and you're welcome to come along.

So don't be shy. Come and join Jeff's incredible journey to find the most intriguing, slithery creatures in the world! The trip begins in Indonesia, then travels to the island of Borneo, where some king cobras reside. Next we'll head to Ecuador, home of a snake that looks like a vine and a boa that squeezes like one.

The fun continues in the Arizona desert, home to rattlesnakes and deadly coral snakes and their harmless mimics. From there, we'll move along to the African republic of Namibia, where the Peringuey's adder and other amazing animals survive in extreme conditions. Finally, we'll land in India, where we'll learn about snake-milking and visit a festival where 100,000 people gather each year to celebrate the planet's largest venomous snake.

Ready to experience the unforgettable creatures that inspire awe throughout the world? Excellent! Grab your gear and join the gang as we head for some of the greatest snake locations anywhere. First stop? Indonesia.

Experience BALI and BORNEO

Bali

Capital: Denpasar.

Area: Bali is an Indonesian island, and covers about 1,930 square miles.

Elevation: The highest point is Gunung Agung, which is 10,249 feet high.

Chief products: Agriculture—rice.

Borneo

Area: The third-largest island in the world, Borneo covers about 287,000 square miles divided up as follows: Indonesian Borneo covers about 210,000 square miles, Sabah (formerly North Borneo) and Sarawak cover about 75,000 square miles, and Brunei's area is about 2,000 square miles.

Elevation: The highest point is Mount Kinabalu, which is 13,431 feet high.

Population: Approximately 12 million people with about 73 percent of the people in Indonesian Borneo, 25 percent in the Malaysian areas, and 2 percent in Brunei.

Chief products: Agriculture—cinnamon, cloves, coffee, cotton, nutmeg, pepper, rice, sugar, and tobacco. Industry—produces oil and rubber.

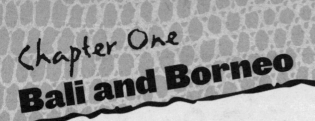

Chapter One
Bali and Borneo

The country of Indonesia is made up of many islands—more than 13,000 in all, including Bali and Borneo. With climates ranging from rain forests to dry plains, the islands of Indonesia boast some of the most fascinating wildlife in the world, including several incredible snake species found nowhere else.

Experience Extra:
About Bali

Just eight degrees south of the equator, the tiny tropical island of Bali has beautiful beaches, majestic mountains, and spectacular wildlife. Bali is also home to many active volcanoes.

Bali's Awesome King

The lush, tropical island of Bali is home to some of the largest, most beautiful, and *deadliest* snakes on the planet. Ready to search for some of these incredible serpents? Let's go!

Finding King Cobra

If you walk in the river running through Bali's Masian Forest late in the afternoon, you just might find a huge snake known as the king—king cobra, that is! This magnificent serpent is the largest venomous snake on the planet, growing up to *20 feet* in length.

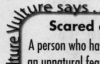

Culture Vulture says...

Scared of Snakes

A person who has an unnatural fear of snakes is called an ophidiophobiac. And an extreme fear of snakes, of course, is an ophidiophobia!

Hail to the King!

The animal is enormous, but it is also called

the king of cobras because it appears fearless. It doesn't flee when it is threatened. The serpent stands its ground, looks its opponent right in the eye, and spreads out a big hood around its head, which makes it look even larger.

Culture Vulture says ...

Charmed, I'm sure

Many of the snakes "hypnotized" by so-called snake charmers are cobras, often king cobras. In recent years, animal rights groups have criticized the ancient tradition of "snake charming" as being cruel to snakes.

To add to its scary pose, the king hisses. But it's no ordinary hiss. The creature produces a hiss that is much lower than that of most snakes—it sounds more like a dog's growl.

And with large amounts of toxic venom, the king cobra is able to defend itself. It eats other serpents, including other cobras, vipers, kraits, and water snakes. That puts this snake right at the top of the serpent food chain!

Getting a Handle on King Cobra

How do you get a handle on king cobra, one of the most poisonous snakes on Earth? Very carefully!

Still, snake experts capture the huge serpent by gently but firmly grabbing it, bare-handed! Jeff says, "You stand there and let them just rise up to you, then sweep and grab." But even the most experienced animal experts sometimes have trouble getting a handle on these superpoisonous serpents!

Bali's Very Own Snake

You can find green pit vipers throughout Southeast Asia, but the *insularis* subspecies is unique to the island of Bali. Al-

Science Note

• Fewer than 10 percent of snakes have dangerous venom, but in a single bite, king cobra can deliver enough venom to kill an elephant—or 10 adult humans!

• Snakes have six rows of teeth.

• Snakes don't have eyelids that move or external ears.

• Most snakes can swallow prey that is triple the size of their own body diameter!

though this bright-green snake has the orange eyes typical of the species, it's different from other green pit vipers because it has a blue, nearly iridescent sheen on its belly.

And although the *insularis* green pit viper is no larger or more poisonous than many other serpents, it is perhaps the most feared snake on the island. Why?

Experience Extra:
About Borneo

Borneo is the third-largest island in the world. Indonesia controls its southern two-thirds, while the northern one-third is controlled by the country of Malaysia. Once completely covered by a dense rain forest, Borneo's environment is now under threat from logging. In fact, about 30 percent of the rain forests of Borneo have been destroyed due to human intervention.

Because the snake is extremely well camouflaged. In fact, this snake looks so much like a vine that many people are bitten each year simply because they didn't notice it hanging in the bush. And when it is disturbed, this snake will bite to defend itself—and it has seriously dangerous venom.

Snake Island!

Near Borneo, there's an island that's almost a legend among herpetologists, the people who study snakes. Its official name is Palaltiga but everyone calls it Snake Island. Why? Because it is *teeming* with serpents!

A Real Sea Serpent?

Yellow-lipped sea kraits aren't known for being aggressive—but they *are* very

Science Note

- Sea kraits have nostril flaps that close to keep out water.

- Some sea kraits bear their young in the water.

- Male sea kraits are much smaller than females.

- Female sea kraits may grow to nearly 5 feet long!

venomous. When Jeff discovered one of these reptiles on Snake Island, he said, "I'm going to handle him as if he's hot. And when I say hot, I mean dangerous!"

Sea kraits spend nearly all of their time in the sea, swimming around coral reefs in search of eels and fish.

JEFF'S JOURNAL:
ON SNAKE ISLAND

"A fellow snake enthusiast once described this island to me. Basically, he said, 'Coming to this place is like being a small mite in the head of Medusa, because all around you squirm these amazing and very venomous snakes.'"

With a flattened tail for paddling, glands for excreting sea salt, and nostrils *on top* of its head so it can breathe while swimming, this snake is well built for life in the open sea.

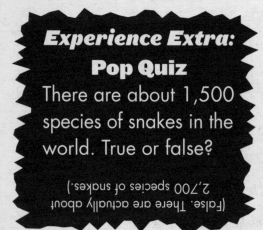

Experience Extra: Pop Quiz

There are about 1,500 species of snakes in the world. True or false?

(False. There are actually about 2,700 species of snakes.)

Powerful Venom

A relative of the deadly cobra, the sea krait has a large, blunt head, short fangs in the front of its mouth—and superstrong venom. This snake produces a neurotoxin in its venom that shuts down the nervous system of its prey.

How powerful is that venom? As Jeff says, "It is said that one teaspoon of venom from this snake is powerful enough to take out about 500 people!" These are definitely not reptiles you want to make mad.

At Home in the Mangrove Swamp

Borneo's mangrove swamps are home to a wide variety of wildlife, including a strikingly beautiful species of venomous snake called a mangrove snake.

The Colors of Danger?!

A mangrove snake has vibrant yellow bands circling its black body. Does that coloring remind you of any other animals?

Here's a clue: Think bees, baby cobras, and

Experience Extra: Rough or Smooth?

Snakes have two types of scales: rough and smooth. Rough scales on snakes are called keeled scales. They give snakes a duller, less shiny appearance, which may help them blend in with their environments.

Science Note

• Mangrove snakes can grow to 6 feet in length—or longer.

• There are seven types of mangrove snakes—the width of their color bands distinguishes them from one another.

• Mangrove snakes are arboreal, which means that they live in trees. And only rarely come down to the ground.

• Although venomous, mangrove snakes can be quite tame and are sometimes used by snake charmers.

certain types of tarantulas! While yellow and black doesn't *always* serve as a warning to predators that an animal is poisonous, in many cases, it does. The color combo of the venomous mangrove snake is nature's way of saying, "Stay away!"

Speaking of *staying away* . . . can you say "anaconda"? They're the biggest—and among the strongest—serpents on the planet! And we'll meet them on our next amazing experience . . . in Ecuador.

Experience ECUADOR

Capital: Quito.

Official language: Spanish.

Official name: Republica del Ecuador (Republic of Ecuador).

Area: 109,484 square miles.

Elevation: The highest point is Chimborazo Volcano in the Andes Mountains, which is 20,561 feet above sea level.

Population: In 2002, the population was estimated at 13,090,000 people. Approximately two-thirds of the population lived in cities and the rest in rural areas.

Chief products: Agriculture—bananas, beef, cacao, corn, milk, coffee, oranges, potatoes, rice, sugarcane, wheat. Fishing—shrimp, herring, mackerel. Forestry—balsa wood. Manufacturing—cement, processed foods, straw hats, textiles. Mining—petroleum.

Money: The basic unit is the United States dollar. One hundred cents equal one dollar.

Chapter Two
Ecuador

Although it is one of South America's smallest countries—just 110 square miles—Ecuador boasts snowcapped mountain peaks, active volcanoes, the Amazon rain forest, tropical beaches, and the Galápagos Islands. With varied climates, Ecuador is home to a wide variety of snakes, including the *biggest* of the big serpents, the mighty anaconda.

Look, No Fangs!

Growing longer than *30* feet, the anaconda is the largest snake on

Experience Extra:
About Ecuador

Ecuador is named for the equator, the imaginary line circling the globe, which divides Earth's northern and southern hemispheres. The equator runs through the northern part of Ecuador.

the planet. Also known as the water boa, the massive, meat-eating snake has no fangs. Instead, this relative of the boa constrictor encircles its prey and *squeezes*.

Science Note

• The largest anaconda ever recorded was 37½ feet long!

• Anacondas give birth to 20 to 40 live babies at a time!

• Anacondas continue to grow their whole lives, getting bigger and bigger each year.

• Young anacondas can take care of themselves soon after birth, hunting small rodents, frogs, fish, and baby birds.

• Although they are carnivores, anacondas don't have teeth and don't chew their food.

Swamp Swimmers?

Anacondas live in tropical, swampy areas of Ecuador and other South American countries. Olive green with large black spots, the snakes are well camouflaged when hanging out in still, shallow water since their coloration makes them very difficult to see. Although slow moving on land, water boas are extremely fast swimmers.

Culture Vulture says …

Deadly to Cattle?

Spanish explorers originally called anacodas *matatoro*, which means "bull killer."

Anacondas are nocturnal, hunting at night and resting during the day. To catch prey, the huge serpent often waits for birds, small mammals, large rodents, and even pigs and deer to come close to the water's edge. Then the snake either grabs its future meal and drowns it underwater . . . or wraps its body around the animal, to kill it by constriction—slowly squeezing it to death.

A Powerful Constrictor

When an anaconda kills by constriction, it wraps itself around its prey. Next it tightens its powerful coils. Each time the prey exhales, the coils tighten around the victim's ribs.

Soon, the anaconda's prey cannot breathe at all, and it dies. Despite tall tales about the enormous snakes, anacondas rarely crush their victims' bones. Instead, they squeeze out the air and prevent their prey from breathing.

Open WIDE!

How can anacondas eat prey far larger than themselves without teeth or fangs? With a special set of jaws. The

JEFF'S JOURNAL:

ON AN ANACONDA THAT HAS JUST EATEN

"This beautiful anaconda has, maybe one or two days ago, eaten something very large which is in the center of her belly right there. She has [a] great lump. She's just sort of resting there, digesting her meal. Beautiful snake. I'd love to further explore this creature, but that big bulge tells me it's just had its meal, and I'm afraid if I move it around too much . . . it's going to vomit up its prey!"

top and bottom jaws of the anaconda are attached with ligaments—bands of stretchy tissue that hold bones in place—that allow the snake to open WIDE . . . and swallow *whole* animals, headfirst. And some of these animals are *huge* in comparison to the snake!

Anacondas don't chew their food. Instead, powerful acids in the snake's stomach digest the prey. After eating a large animal, an anaconda digests for several weeks.

Is It a Vine . . . or a Snake?

If you look up in the Ecuadoran rain forest, you may just see something that's long, thin,

Science Note

• Vine snakes have such flexible bodies that they can coil into a ball.

• The scientific name for the green vine snake comes from the ancient Greek word *oxybelis*, which means "sharp" or "pointed," and from the Latin word *fulgidus*, for "shining," which refers to the animal's bright shade of green.

• Because of its light weight, the vine snake is able to lift half of its body into the air!

• Lizards and small birds make up the green vine snake's diet. Larger birds and mammals prey on the green vine snake.

• The creatures are diurnal, which means they are active during daylight.

green, and draped between tree boughs. Is it a vine? No . . . it's a vine *snake.*

Incredible Camouflage!

Vine snakes are arboreal—in other words, they live in trees. Barely as thick as a person's finger but growing to more than 6 feet in length, the vine snake is an especially long, slim serpent.

JEFF'S JOURNAL:
ON A GREEN VINE SNAKE

"It just hangs out. You could walk by and never know that this tail was attached to a 2-meter snake. You would think it was the extension of a vine or the tendril of a philodendron. But it is a wonderful snake. Great stuff, Ecuador."

In fact, these snakes are *so* long and slender that it is easy to confuse them with their surroundings. This serpent's camouflage is its best defense because it looks exactly like the vines and creepers where it spends its time. Slow moving, with rear fangs—grooved fangs located at the back of the mouth—and mild venom, the green vine snake spends its days lying in wait for lizards and young birds.

When frightened, vine snakes may camouflage themselves even further by staying very still or swaying from side to side in the breeze, like a plant stem. If a predator threatens, the "vine" suddenly becomes a very large *snake*. It puffs up the front of its body and opens its mouth wide.

Cool Convergence!

Even in places that are thousands of miles from South America, like India and Southeast Asia, Jeff has found snakes that look exactly like the Ecuadoran vine snake.

But these snakes aren't related to one another! This phenomenon is called convergence.

As Jeff says, "Convergence is when two species, in two different parts of the world, evolve similar survival skills or adaptations to meet the challenges of the environment. They come from unique origins; they don't share a similar genetic or biological path. But what they have in common is they survive the same way, whether that's eating a particular resource or avoiding a predator."

In other words, the two species may have had nothing in common to start, but their shared ways of *surviving* result in convergence. And it eventually makes them similar to one another!

The Amazon's Very Own Tree Boa!

Ranging from gray and black to bright reds, oranges, and yellows, the Amazon tree boa appears in a wide variety of colors and patterns. Moving between the

Science Note

- The average Amazon tree boa grows to between 4 and 5 feet in length.

- A female Amazon tree boa of one color may produce a litter of young with many other colors and patterns.

- Each Amazon tree boa possesses a pair of spurs that are remnants of an ancient pelvic girdle. Pelvic girdles are basin-shaped bones that connect the body and the legs. Males have larger spurs than females.

- Amazon tree boas are able to hold on to tree limbs with their tails—and dangle!

ground and trees along the Amazon River, these snakes are known for being ag-gressive—at *squeezing* their prey.

Slim Constrictors!

Amazon tree boas have distinctive bulky heads, thin necks, and slim bodies—especially slim for a boa. They eat rodents, lizards, and insects. (Since Jeff was being attacked by mosquitoes in the place where he found the serpent, that's *great* news!)

Like other snakes, the Amazon tree boa uses its forked tongue to pick up chemical "clues" in the air and on objects. Those clues lead the serpent to prey—and *away* from predators.

An Indian rock python puts the squeeze on Jeff.

King cobra

A rattlesnake uses its rattle to say, "Back off!"

Green vine snake

Yellow-lipped sea krait

Jeff holds a mangrove snake.
Check out its gorgeous colors!

Capturing a rattlesnake—not a time for an attack of nerves.

Rattlesnake

Jeff uses a snake stick to manipulate a rattlesnake without hurting either the snake or himself.

Jeff uses cotton bags to move snakes safely.

This king snake looks like a coral snake but it's not poisonous.

Black mamba

Coral snake

Jeff carefully holds a king cobra.

The opening of the Nag Panchami cobra festival.

A snake's venom is collected in a glass. Later it will be used to make antivenin.

Russell's viper

Some snakes may produce only a few drops of venom per milking.

Elliptical Eyes

If you can picture a cat's eyes, you can imagine the eyes of an Amazon tree boa. The snake has elliptical pupils, similar to the shape of a lemon or an almond.

The snake's pupils get wider or narrower (think fatter or skinnier lemon) depending on how much light is

JEFF'S JOURNAL:
ON ELLIPTICAL PUPILS

"Look at those eyes. They have elliptical pupils. During the nighttime, those pupils widen. During the daytime, they're just little slits, cutting out as much of the light as possible."

JEFF'S JOURNAL:
ON ENCOUNTERING
AN AMAZON TREE BOA

"I do believe my eyes spy a tree boa . . . Oh, my gosh—isn't that beautiful? It's an arboreal boa. I'll tell you what, I'm being eaten alive, I'm inhaling mosquitoes, so I'm going to bring this guy back to my camp, and then tomorrow, I'm going to show him to you, show you how beautiful he looks in the daylight!"

available. When the pupils are wide, the maximum amount of light is let in. Narrow pupils mean less light is admitted. The pupils work a little like natural "sunglasses" for the serpent.

It's time to head north, for an experience with some of the fantastic snakes of the southwestern United States. Next stop, the Arizona desert—otherwise known as "rattlesnake country!"

Experience ARIZONA

Statehood: Feb. 14, 1912, the 48th state.

State capital: Phoenix, the capital of Arizona since 1889.

Area: 114,007 square miles.

Elevation: The highest point is Humphreys Peak, 12,633 feet above sea level.

Population: 5,130,632 people, with 87 percent living in cities and the remaining 13 percent in rural areas.

Chief Products: Agriculture—beef cattle, cotton, lettuce, melons, milk. Manufacturing—computer components, transportation equipment, chemicals, fabricated metal products. Mining—copper, gold.

Chapter Three
Arizona

A rizona is a land of extremes. Temperatures climb from below freezing to higher than 110 degrees Fahrenheit in a matter of hours. Not surprisingly, many of the animals that thrive in the Arizona desert are tough reptiles—including many snakes.

Rattlesnake Country

The Arizona desert is home to an American original—the true rattlesnake! Found only in North, Central, and South America, rattlesnakes are known for making a distinctive sound with the rattles on the end of their tails and for being some of the most venomous North American snakes.

If you follow Jeff, you'll experience some of the *loudest* serpents around.

Experience Extra:
About Arizona

Arizona's habitats and ecosystems include parched desert alongside areas that have lots of grasses and trees. In fact, these ecosystems may be one and the same. In the desert, months pass without a drop of rain, then suddenly, there's a monsoon— with near floodlike conditions. The vast landscape of Arizona means a great variety of creatures are able to survive in some of the toughest, most challenging conditions anywhere.

Rattlers: A Short History

Why do rattlesnakes have rattles? Rattlesnakes developed their rattles as a protective device. Rattlesnakes lie in the sun to get warm, and they blend in with their surroundings. Unfortunately for the snakes, this means that they can get stepped on by larger animals. As Jeff explains,

Culture Vulture says . . .

Rattlesnake History

American colonists added a rattlesnake to their flag to send a message to the British during the Revolutionary War. The snake had 13 rattles, one for each of the original American colonies. The message? "Don't tread on me!"

"Rattlesnakes developed rattles as a warning mechanism so large-hoofed creatures wouldn't come on in and stomp on them!"

Rattlesnakes usually vibrate their rattles to threaten predators,

Experience Extra: Pop Quiz?

A sidewinding rattlesnake lives in the American Southwest. True or false?

(True.)

but some scientists believe that smaller types of rattlesnakes may use their rattles to *attract* birds and other prey. The high-pitched sound produced by smaller snakes may sound like the buzzing of an insect to birds, which lures them into range so that the snake can strike!

Science Note

• The rattles on a rattlesnake grow one segment at a time—every time the snake sheds its skin. They are made up of keratin, the same material in human fingernails. The older the snake, the more rattles.

• Snakes vibrate their tail rattles like a person shaking a rattle.

• Rattlesnakes eat rodents, birds, lizards, and other small animals.

• Rattlesnakes belong to a family of snakes called pit vipers. Pits on their faces let them sense heat to find warm-blooded prey.

• Some rattlesnakes can swim, and they hold their rattles above water to keep them dry!

The Mighty Mojave!

The Mojave rattlesnake is North America's most venomous snake—and is among the most deadly serpents in the world. It produces both a hemotoxin, which attacks the circulatory system and the internal organs, and a neurotoxin, which attacks the nervous system and causes death by heart failure and paralysis.

So a single bite from a Mojave rattlesnake destroys both tissues *and* nerves. Ouch!

Western Diamondback, "Combat Dancer!"

The western diamondback is named for the diamond-shaped patches that run along its back. As thick as a man's wrist, it is one of the largest and longest snakes in North America. If fact, some diamondbacks have been known to reach 7 feet in length. The diamondback is one of the most dangerous snakes in America, with *seriously* strong venom!

But it is also one of the most unusual snakes around because of the "combat dance" that male

Culture Vulture says . . .

Symbolic Snake

The western diamondback rattlesnake has been a symbol of the American Southwest for a long time. It has been a part of Native American mythology, appearing on pottery and other artifacts since pre-Columbian times!

JEFF'S JOURNAL:
MEETING A BABY
DIAMONDBACK

"We've just discovered a baby diamondback rattlesnake. You can see her beautiful
diamonds running along the back of her
body like that. Now, I've got to hold this
snake very carefully, because she is
brand-new to this world, extremely fragile. I don't want to damage her in any
way. I also have to keep in mind that even
though she's maybe a month old, she is
armed, she's venomous. They're born venomous, okay, and that venom is potent
and I could be injured if she bites me. So
I've just got to hold her very carefully!"

western diamondbacks perform to win mates. When two males meet, they raise their heads off the ground, press bellies, and begin to wrestle each other. The match is over when one snake gives up and slithers away—while the victor gets to stay with the female.

JEFF'S JOURNAL:
ON THE RATTLESNAKES' REPUTATION

"They have a pretty nasty reputation, but I don't believe that reputation is completely deserved. This animal is only going to bite you if you mess with it, if you step on it. And I once read an interesting study about rattlesnakes, and something like 70 percent of all rattlesnake bites involve alcohol. And I don't think it was the rattlesnake that was drinking!"

A Built-in Tool?

Jeff also encountered a very unusual snake in the Arizona desert. This particular snake is a nocturnal creature and has a very useful *nose!*

The Amazing Long-nosed Snake

This particular snake has three different colors on its body. It has "a cream-colored body with black and red or pink splotches." As if this weren't enough to make the snake different, it also has a very long nose—for a snake. And this long, pointed nose is extremely useful as the snake hunts for its favorite foods such as small rodents, lizards and their eggs, and even small snakes. Using its nose like a hoe, the snake can push its way into the nests or dens of these animals.

During the day, the long-nosed snake can also use its nose to burrow between rocks or underground, where it can hide from the sun, predators, and humans. As Jeff explains, "By having a sort of elongated, narrow muzzle, it has a natural tool that it can use to either burrow into the earth or wedge its way into rocks."

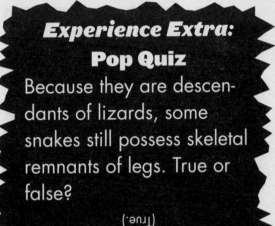

Experience Extra: Pop Quiz

Because they are descendants of lizards, some snakes still possess skeletal remnants of legs. True or false?

(True.)

This is a fascinating and unusual snake, but Arizona has lots of cool snakes. Come along as Jeff meets another one.

King of the Mountain?

The Arizona mountain king snake is one of the most striking snakes around. While this king snake isn't very big—rarely exceeding 42 inches in length—it is very noticeable. And that's because of its bright bands of

JEFF'S JOURNAL:
ON A SHEDDING ARIZONA MOUNTAIN KING SNAKE

"Isn't that beautiful? Have you ever seen a snake with such colors? In fact, this one can be even more beautiful because he's getting ready to shed. I know he's ready to shed because his belly is blue. That's called the opaque cycle. Basically, what happens is the skin is pushed off their body and they exfoliate, just literally shed their skin off. This is the mountain king snake—the Arizona mountain king snake. Brilliant bands of red and yellow and they're even brighter with that black!"

red, yellow, and black. These bands are not only beautiful but also serve as a warning to other creatures. These colors are a sign of danger! But, as Jeff says, the colors on this king snake are just a bluff. Although the Arizona mountain king snake closely resembles other very venomous snakes, it's harmless to humans.

But the Arizona mountain king snake *is* a threat to other snakes, lizards, and rodents. It grabs its prey tightly, coiling around the prey's body, and then constricts. Once the prey suffocates, the king snake swallows it whole.

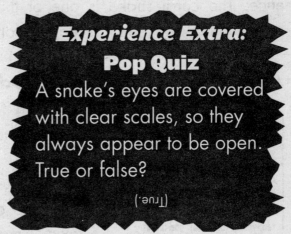

Experience Extra: Pop Quiz

A snake's eyes are covered with clear scales, so they always appear to be open. True or false?

(True.)

Experiencing Coral Snakes

The Arizona coral snake looks very much like the Arizona mountain king snake. There is one *key* difference: The coral snake is one of the *most poisonous* snakes around, as Jeff has learned for himself!

Arizona Coral Snake: An Introduction

> **Science Note**
>
> The Arizona mountain king snake is often mistaken for the highly poisonous (and VERY dangerous) coral snake. Small and thin, both kinds of serpent have bands of red, yellow (or white), and black!
>
> An old saying about the serpents' color bands can help people tell the difference between harmless milk and king snakes and deadly coral snakes:
>
> "Red touch yellow, kill a fellow.
> Red touch black, venom lack!"
>
> Of course, if you encounter a snake, the best advice of all is: DON'T TOUCH IT!

Although it has tiny fangs, is usually slender, and is only about 20 inches long, the coral snake falls in the same category of deadly neurotoxic snakes as cobras, kraits, and mambas!

Arizona coral snakes live in rocky, desert areas, usually staying hidden underground during the day.

At night, they come out to hunt their prey. Coral snakes eat small lizards, snakes and other reptiles, and amphibians. When disturbed, this serpent often will hide its head in its coils . . . and wave its tail at its predator! But on occasion, it will bite.

Encounters with the Deadly Coral Snake

How dangerous are coral snakes? Jeff was bitten once by a coral snake—and nearly *died.* It happened while he was a graduate student working in Belize, a country in Central America. Jeff was in the jungle when he was bitten, and it took about three and a half hours to get to a place where he could re-

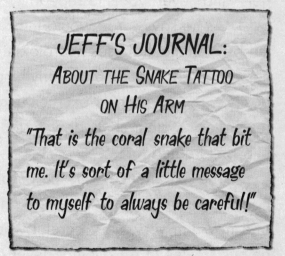

JEFF'S JOURNAL:
About the Snake Tattoo
on His Arm
"That is the coral snake that bit me. It's sort of a little message to myself to always be careful!"

ceive antivenin (a treatment for the bite, also called venolim). Since the venom in coral snakes is capable of

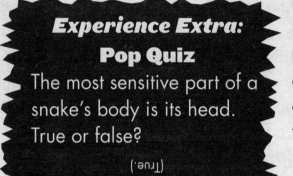

Experience Extra:
Pop Quiz

The most sensitive part of a snake's body is its head. True or false?

(True.)

killing a person in four or five hours, Jeff was definitely in serious trouble that time!

It was an experience that he'll never forget—and never wants to repeat!

As he says, "You would think that if you were bitten by a snake that uses neurotoxin that it would kill the nerve and you wouldn't feel anything, but it was the opposite. . . . The pain is excruciating!" Eventually, your respiratory system shuts down, and you can die if the bite isn't treated.

The experience with the coral snake was an important lesson for Jeff. "I got too cavalier that moment, and now I'm very, very careful when I work with venomous snakes in an attempt never to repeat that. . . . I would certainly never want anyone to watch my show and think that . . . they can go out and capture a venomous snake!"

It's time to take off for another desert—this time in Africa. Namibia is the spectacular setting for many different kinds of serpents including the huge, swift black mamba, the deadliest snake in the world!

Experience NAMIBIA

Capital: Windhoek.

Official language: English.

Official name: Republic of Namibia.

Area: 318,261 square miles.

Elevation: The highest point is Brandberg, which is 8,465 feet above sea level.

Population: In 2002, the population was estimated at 1,768,000 people. Approximately 73 percent of the population lived in rural areas, and the remaining 27 percent lived in cities.

Chief products: Agriculture—cattle, fish, sheep, corn, millet, vegetables. Mining—copper, diamonds, lead, uranium oxide, zinc.

Money: The basic units are the Namibian dollar and South African rand.

Chapter Four
Namibia

The republic of Namibia on Africa's southwestern coast features some of the continent's most diverse natural habitats. It's a land of extremes—from the massive, arid Namib and Kalihari Deserts to plains and

Experience Extra:
About Namibia

When Namibia gained its independence from South Africa in 1990, it became the first country in the world to incorporate protection of the environment into its constitution! About 14 percent of Namibia's land is protected, including nearly all of the Namib Desert coastal region!

woodlands. The tough terrain of Namibia is host to a fascinating *sidewinding* serpent—and the fastest snake on the planet!

Slithering by Sidewinding!

In the extraordinarily sunny, sandy, and dry Namib Desert, animals have adapted to the harsh climate.

The venomous sidewinding snake, also known as Peringuey's adder, exhibits several of the ingenious ways that a creature can survive in the extremes of the African desert.

"S" Is for Sidewinder!

The desert sidewinder is named for the way it moves. Forming an S shape with its body, it slithers gracefully and quickly in a curving movement across the sand, leaving a wavelike pattern behind it.

Why does the serpent move sideways? Some scientists believe side-winding cuts down on its contact with hot sand and pro-tects its skin. Side-winding may also allow the animal to move more quickly over sand.

At Home in the Sand!

> ## Science Note
>
> • Two species of sidewinder snakes live in the Namib Desert: the Peringuey's adder and the Namaqua dwarf adder.
>
> • The Peringuey's adder is only about 1 foot long.
>
> • The color of the Peringuey's adder closely matches the quartz sand grains in the Namib Desert, providing excellent camouflage.
>
> • Its dark tail tip contrasts with the color of the sand, attracting the attention of potential prey!
>
> • The sidewinder is diurnal, which means it is active during the day.

At dawn, fog from the coast of Namibia rolls in to the Namib Desert. That's when the Peringuey's adder is out, collecting water—on its skin, that is. Later, when the water condenses, the snake licks off the water droplets. This is just one way that this snake survives in the harsh conditions.

Another survival technique involves hiding in the sand. For most of the day, the snake burrows into the sand to protect itself against the scorching sun. Only its

JEFF'S JOURNAL:
ABOUT THE POWERFUL PERINGUEY'S ADDER

"He looks so diminuitive and fragile, but he packs a potent bite. He is a viper. And as with most species of vipers, the venom is designed to both kill the prey and destroy the tissue of the prey to make the digestion process that much easier. And even a creature this small could potentially be deadly to a human being my size."

eyes—located on top of its triangular head—are visible above the surface. This way, the Peringuey's adder can keep an eye out for potential prey—or predators—while keeping cool.

The Fastest Snake

It's not really black, but the black mamba is Africa's most venomous snake. A relative of the cobra, it is a *huge* serpent, growing longer than 12 feet!

And the black mamba moves fast. In fact, it's the fastest snake in the world!

Built for Speed—and to Stand!

Black mambas race along the ground with their heads raised, but that doesn't slow them down at all. These snakes can

Culture Vulture says . . .

Faster Than a Speeding Snake?

In Africa, the speed of the black mamba is legendary. Many tales describe how frequently the snakes overtake humans and then bite them! However, in reality, most people can outrun and escape a snake . . . no matter how swift it is.

achieve slithering speeds between 7 and 12 miles per

hour, reaching speeds of up to *15* miles per hour for short distances when chasing prey!

These snakes usually flee from the humans they encounter. However, when a black mamba feels threatened, it may become very aggressive . . . and may stand its ground.

Science Note

• Black mambas never build their own nests. They simply move into rock crevices, hollow trees, or shelters abandoned by other animals.

• Black mambas will stay in the same shelter for years if undisturbed.

• A black mamba may lay up to 14 eggs at one time. Newborn black mambas measure 18 to 24 inches.

• In captivity, black mambas have lived up to 12 years!

When it's agitated, a black mamba raises its head and body 3 or 4 feet into the air. It spreads a flat hood and opens its mouth wide. When it strikes, the snake quickly bites many times, delivering super-potent venom.

Incredible Venom!

How strong is a black mamba's venom? The snake produces between 100 and 120 milligrams—about 20 drops—of neurotoxic venom (the type of venom that stops people from breathing). Two drops of black mamba venom is a lethal dose for an adult human!

As Jeff explains, "If this creature were to land a bite on me, I would have anywhere from a half an hour to four hours to start receiving antivenin. If you don't get the antivenin, you're going to die."

JEFF'S JOURNAL:
ON MEETING A BLACK MAMBA

"I am in seventh heaven right now. For herpetologists to see this creature face-to-face, it doesn't get any better.... When you first think of the mamba, you think of dangerous, cruel, ornery and ugly ... but, in fact, it's a spectacular creature. When respected, it's a creature that really brings home the beauty and the magnificence of Africa!"

Fortunately, antivenin is now available! As recently as 40 years ago, it didn't exist, and black mamba bites were 100 percent fatal.

A Useful Serpent

The black mamba may be the most-feared snake in all of Africa, but it's also very important. Like many snakes, the black mamba plays a major role in controlling rodent populations. It eats rats, mice, squirrels, and voles.

Science Note

• Black mambas usually have very dark olive, brown, or gray scales, black speckles, and a grayish-white belly.

• Most black mambas measure between 8 and 12 feet long, though some get as long as 14 feet!

• Mambas have very long fangs, which are useful for biting through birds' feathers!

• These creatures spend most of their time on the ground, but they will climb up trees to escape predators or search for prey.

• Black mambas live in savannahs, woodlands, and rocky regions, nesting in tree hollows, rock crevices, or mammal burrows.

And while the superstrong venom of black mambas may be deadly to humans, it may turn out to be useful as well. Scientists are studying the snake's venom for possible use as a painkiller. It has also been used to aid blood coagulation (clotting), which helps people heal from injuries.

Black mambas aren't the only useful serpents around. In the next experience, we'll meet some spectacular serpents. They are so helpful to humans that they're the focus of an *entire* festival . . . in India!

Experience INDIA

Capital: New Delhi.

Principal official language: Hindi.

Official name: Bharat Ganarajya (Republic of India).

Area: 1,269,346 square miles.

Elevation: The highest point is Kanchenjunga, which is 28,208 feet above sea level.

Population: In 2001, the population was 1,027,015,247 people. Approximately 72 percent lived in rural areas and the remaining 28 percent lived in cities.

Chief products: Agriculture—bananas, beans, chickpeas, coconuts, cotton, jute, mangoes, onions, oranges, peanuts, pepper, potatoes, rice, sesame seeds, sugarcane, tea, wheat. Manufacturing—bicycles, brassware and silverware, cement, chemicals, clothing, fertilizer, iron and steel, leather goods, machinery, medicines, motor vehicles, paper, rugs, sewing machines, sugar, wood products. Mining—coal, iron ore, limestone, petroleum.

Money: The basic unit is the rupee. One hundred paise equal one rupee.

Chapter Five

India

From the snows of the Himalayan mountains to sunny beaches, from parched deserts to humid jungles, India is a land with an incredible variety of ecosystems. Located in southern Asia, the country boasts more than 230 types of snakes!

Meet Russell's Viper, Medicine Maker!

The Russell's viper is a large, very toxic snake—which is said to be very excitable. With venom that is 60 times more poisonous than rattlesnake venom, Russell's vipers are responsible for more snakebite deaths than any other serpent because they strike quickly without warning or reason. But thanks to one community in India, the creature is also helping to save more people than ever.

Experience Extra:
About India

With a long tradition of respect for all living things, India is the scene of many fascinating relationships between humans and animals—and serpents play a starring role! From communities that thrive through capturing and milking venomous serpents to an important festival dedicated to cobras, it's a country that uses, honors, and celebrates snakes like no other.

Milking Russell's Vipers!

The Irula people in the Indian village of Anjuna have been experts at producing snakeskin leather for centuries. Now, they have a new business using their snake-hunting and -handling skills. Their harvest? Venom that is used to make antivenin to help people survive snakebites.

Making Antivenin: Milking Snakes

How do you "milk" venom from a snake that might be *deadly*? (Hint: Do not try this at home!)

> ### Science Note
> • The average Russell's viper is about 3 feet long.
>
> • The Russell's viper is brown, with a long, triangular head, large nostrils, and very big fangs.
>
> • The snake coils and hisses when disturbed. If excited, its body vibrates and produces a rasping sound by rubbing scales from one part of its body on another.

Holding the poisonous snake very securely over a venom-collection container is *key*. (You don't want to injure the snake!) As Jeff put it, "Then, there we go. Just let him do it on his own!"

This means dealing with a very angry Russell's viper. The snake shakes violently—but bites into the container just as it is supposed to. And voilá—*venom*!

Making Medicine

Once it's collected, the venom is dried so that it becomes crystalized. The dehydrated venom is then

JEFF'S JOURNAL:
MILKING THE RUSSELL'S VIPER

"This is the first time I've actually milked a Russell's viper. . . . And I'm trying to look cool. . . . This snake doesn't produce as much venom as some of the other ones. But you saw the nature of the snake. Extremely, extremely cantankerous, not a snake you would want to mess with in the field. Because I got a little venom on my hand, I've got to give it a rinse because I can actually feel it tingle!"

mixed with a hemoglobin (a protein in red blood cells) of a horse. This mixture is used as an antivenin—the antidote for snakebites.

Science Note

- Indian rock pythons can weigh up to 300 pounds!

- Birds, fish, reptiles, rodents, and mammals (including large creatures such as deer and leopards) make up the Indian rock python's diet.

- Indian rock pythons lay as many as 60 eggs at one time.

- Heat-sensing pits on their lips help Indian rock pythons pinpoint warm-blooded prey. They can either wait for prey in trees or hunt on the move.

The Indian Rock Python

At one time, the Indian rock python was very common throughout India. But because of habitat loss and hunting, it is becoming rare! Fortunately, Jeff got to experience one of these amazing reptiles when he found one hanging from a tree!

Squeezed to Meet You!

The Indian rock python is one of the world's largest snakes, reaching anywhere from 13 to 20 feet long. Nonvenomous, pythons kill their prey by constricting, or squeezing. One even mistook Jeff's *arm* for a possible meal.

JEFF'S JOURNAL:
POWERFUL PYTHON!

"Beautiful snake. She's checking my blood pressure. Well, actually, this is how she protects herself. If she were to be attacked by a predator, she would first bite, then wrap around, but this hug that she's doing, this squeeze, most importantly, is the way she kills her prey. My left arm is turning purple because she's literally cutting off the blood flow from my body to my arm!"

Calling All Cobras!

Each year, more than 100,000 people make a trek to the tiny village of Battis Shirala for the festival of Nag

Panchami. The people come to worship, dance, and take part in special competitions. The contestants? *Cobras* they've collected!

The Snake-Human Connection

Snakes are often feared, even hated, by people in various cultures. But throughout India and elsewhere in the world, snakes are extremely important because they eat rats and mice that destroy crops. At the festival, farmers over-

Science Note

• Sometimes longer than 18 feet, the king cobra is the largest venomous snake on the planet.

• Snake venom is highly specialized saliva.

• As a poison, king cobra venom is 40 times more powerful than cyanide!

• In a single strike, a cobra can deliver enough poison to kill more than *10 men*, or a large elephant!

Experience Extra: About Nag Panchami

The Hindu festival of Nag Panchami is dedicated to the serpent Ananta. Lord Vishnu, a Hindu god, is said to recline on the snake's coils!

come their fear of venomous snakes and show their gratitude to the helpful creatures in a way that brings people and snakes together.

Paying Tribute to Cobras

In the Hindu religion, the cobra is known as Nag. Nag is the symbol of Shiva, the god of destruction of nature.

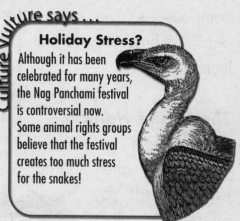

Culture Vulture says ...

Holiday Stress?
Although it has been celebrated for many years, the Nag Panchami festival is controversial now. Some animal rights groups believe that the festival creates too much stress for the snakes!

The cobra is a physically powerful creature, and it is thought to be spiritually powerful as well! As Jeff explains, that is why a live cobra is brought into the homes of believers and treated as a welcome guest. In a special ceremony, the woman of the house stands before the cobra and presents an offering of food to Nag. The male leader places garlands around the cobra's neck and sprinkles bright red powder on the creature. After the indoor ceremony, the celebration moves into the streets.

JEFF'S JOURNAL:
ON PAYING TRIBUTE TO NAG

"I love experiences like this, where not only do you have a chance to travel to an exotic place and learn about the wildlife that you'd find there, but you also get to witness just a little window into the culture that helps to make that land very rich. And in this case we're in India, we're learning about the snakes, but we also have a chance to experience the relation-ship between people and snakes!"

A Serpentine Parade

To kick off the festivities, a long parade winds its way through the streets of Battis Shirala! And real snakes are an important part of the fun!

People transport snakes in clay pots. They display them on floats. Some are even carried *by hand* through the village, accompanied by loud, festive music and cheers!

Cobra Competitions

In the two weeks before the Nag Panchami festival begins, teams across India collect cobras. At a recent festival, 65 teams collected cobras to compete in two categories. The first competition was the longest cobra. The other? The heaviest snake at the festival!

Experience Extra: Pop Quiz

The word *ophidiophobiac* means a person who enjoys working or playing with snakes. True or false?

(False! An ophidiophobiac is a person who has an unnatural fear of snakes! As Jeff says, harvesting venom from snakes could be the ultimate nightmare for an ophidiophobiac!)

Snake Handling

The people who compete with cobras at the Nag Panchami festival are experienced snake handlers. They know that a cobra can only strike out *horizontally* the distance it can raise itself *vertically*.

They also know that a cobra will only strike when its hood is extended. As Jeff says, the men who handle the snakes at the festival do not fear them. They believe a mutual respect between serpent and human exists and

JEFF'S JOURNAL:
On Celebrating Cobras
"Well, this is it. It's my last diary entry in India.... I just finally finished at the Nag Panchami festival. An extraordinary experience. Not for the claustrophobic. Basically, a squirming wall of humanity. India was a great adventure. I'm glad I came!"

that the festival honoring these reptiles ensures this ever-lasting bond.

An Incredible Party!

With more than 100,000 people attending, the Nag Panchami festival is a *huge* party! The streets of Battis Shirala fill with crowds of people dancing, music blares, and snakes appear wherever you turn. For someone like Jeff, it's a remarkable experience and the perfect end to another experience.

From India to Namibia, from the Arizona desert to the Amazon rain forest, we've explored the most fascinating serpents in the world.

But hold on a second! Want to see how much you remember about the journey through the world of snakes that you've experienced with *The Jeff Corwin Experience?* Take the quiz to find out.

SNAKES!

As you read this book, you experienced some of the most remarkable serpents throughout the world! So what did you *learn* by hanging with Jeff? Find out by taking this quick quiz on some of these amazing animals.

1. The old rhyme about venomous snakes goes, "Red touch yellow . . ."
a. "kill a fellow!"
b. "always mellow!"
c. "means, 'Say hello!'"

2. To pay tribute during the Nag Panchami festival, believers
a. place decorative garlands around the cobra's neck.
b. create jeweled tail covers for the cobra.
c. sprinkle bright blue dust on the cobra.

3. Anacondas can grow to up to
a. 40 feet long.
b. 30 feet long.
c. 50 feet long.

4. The Irula people harvest snake venom to make
a. perfume.
b. dye.
c. snakebite antidote.

5. While swimming, sea kraits are able to
a. close their eyes.
b. close their ears.
c. close their nostrils.

6. In the Namib Desert, snakes get moisture from
a. digging down to deep springs.
b. fog that condenses on their skin.
c. cacti.

7. Venom from a single bite of a king cobra could kill an animal as large as
a. a cat.
b. a tiger.
c. an elephant.

8. The green vine snake has
a. rear fangs.
b. rattles.
c. blue eyes.

9. Rattlesnake rattles are made of the same material found in
a. teeth.
b. fingernails.
c. sand.

10. On average, a black mamba can move at a speed of
a. 7 to 12 miles per hour.
b. 15 to 20 miles per hour.
c. 3 to 6 miles per hour.

Answers: 1.a, 2.a, 3.b, 4.c, 5.c, 6.b, 7.c, 8.a, 9.b, 10.a.

1–3 Correct: You must be an ophidiophobiac. Go back and reread the book to help you get over your fear of snakes. Remember, don't bother snakes and they won't bother you.

4–6 Correct: Not bad. You aren't ready to join the *Experience* crew yet, but with a little more reading you will be soon.

7–10 Correct: Congratulations! You have all the makings of a future herpetologist (that's someone who studies reptiles and amphibians).

GLOSSARY

Agile [A-juhl]: able to move easily or quickly.

Antidote [AN-tih-doat]: a remedy to counteract the effects of poison.

Antivenin [an-tih-VEH-nuhn]: an antidote for venom.

Arboreal [ahr-BOHR-ee-uhl]: dwelling in trees.

Cantankerous [kan-TANK-kuhr-uhs]: grouchy.

Diurnal [DIE-uhr-nuhl]: active during the day.

Hemoglobin [HEE-muh-glow-buhn]: a protein containing red blood cells.

Hemotoxin [HEE-muh-tahx-uhn]: a poison that attacks the circulatory system and the internal organs.

Ligament [LIH-guh-muhnt]: a band of stretchy tissue that connects bones.

Neurotoxin [noor-oh-TAHK-suhn]: a poison that attacks the nervous system and causes death by heart failure and paralysis.

Nocturnal [NAHK-tuhr-nuhl]: active at night.

Ophidiophobiac [OH-fihd-ee-oh-fohb-ee-ak]: a person who has a severe fear of snakes.

Toxic [TAHK-sihk]: poisonous.

Venom [VEH-nuhm]: poison produced by some snakes, insects, and spiders.

All photographs copyright © Discovery Communications, Inc. unless noted below.